Laugh in any storm: The secrets to a happy marriage

A marriage is a union that celebrates a beautiful love story. Loving, lifelong companionship.

The first step is to choose a good wife/husband.

Love one another.

It's in the nature of a person.

Act as one.

A partner has to want to make a marriage successful.

Respect each other.

Pray together, serve God together.

Serve each other.

Pray for each other.

Have a personal relationship with God as a couple.

Put God first and each other next.

God is your first priority and secondly you are each other's priority.

Be romantic.

Be spontaneous.

Focus on family.

Be adventurous.

Be of merit to each other.

Submit to each other.

Serve each other.

Have date nights.

Make time for each other.

Eat well.

Have good night's sleep.

Agree on values, goals and ground rules in the marriage earlier on.

Agree on important things and things that matter.

Have a discussion, not an argument.

Appreciate communication.

Make amends when you argue.

Learn to laugh together.

Foster curiosity in the marriage.

Make time for each other.

Be appreciative.

Share some hobbies together.

And have hobbies separately.

Have fortitude.

Offer thoughtful advice.

Never criticise.

Complement each other.

Never look for faults.

Be fair.

Share everything.

Take holidays often and breaks.

Relax and enjoy each other.

Be patient.

Be compassionate.

Be kind and sweet to each other.

Smile often.

Celebrate each other.

Celebrate wedding anniversaries, weddings and birthdays.

Support each other's passions.

Fulfil each other's needs.

Be selfless.

Have good judgement.

Have common sense.

Practice tactfulness.

Have a moderate temperament.

Be indulgent.

Be hospitable to each other.

Host each other.

Loyalty is worth it.

Support each other.

Direct and guide each other kindly.

Be empathetic.

Look in the same direction.

Foster a harmonious marriage.

Show affection often.

Keep the sparkle alive.

Be diplomatic.

Keep a loving home.

Whatever you do in the marriage should be reciprocal.

Be diligent.

Practice forgiveness.

75

Be modest.

Practice humility.

Be down to earth.

Create a safe space to have difficult conversations and resolve these without laying blame.

Nurture the life partner in each other.

Be helpful.

Praise God together.

Be patient.

Think together.

Make memories.

Keep showing up to the marriage.

Fall in love with the same person often.

Be passionate.

See the goodness in each other.

Work as a team.

Build trust in the marriage.

Marriage is lifelong friendship.

Most of all, enjoy the journey.

Printed in Poland
by Amazon Fulfillment
Poland Sp. z o.o., Wrocław
02 October 2022

c0e2cc6d-e100-4433-a180-5a108e74682dR02